STICK UP
FOR
YOURSELF!

**Every Kid's Guide to
Personal Power and
Positive Self-Esteem**

Gershen Kaufman, Ph.D.
Lev Raphael, Ph.D.

Edited by Pamela Espeland

Free Spirit ®
PUBLISHING

Library of Congress Cataloging-in-Publication Data

Kaufman, Gershen.
    Stick up for yourself! : every kid's guide to personal power and positive self-esteem / by Gershen Kaufman and Lev Raphael.
    p. cm.
    Summary: Discusses problems facing young people such as making choices, learning about and liking yourself, and solving problems.
    ISBN 0-915793-17-2
    1. Assertiveness (Psychology)—Juvenile literature. 2. Control (Psychology)—Juvenile literature. 3. Self-respect—Juvenile literature. [1. Assertiveness (Psychology) 2. Self-respect.] I. Raphael, Lev. II. Title.
BF575.A85K38 1990
158'.1'0834—dc20   89-28642
                                          CIP
                                          AC

Printed in the United States of America
10 9 8 7 6 5 4 3 2

Cover and text design by MacLean & Tuminelly
Illustrated by Jackie Urbanovic

FREE SPIRIT PUBLISHING INC.
400 First Avenue North, Suite 616
Minneapolis, MN 55401
(612) 338-2068

Acknowledgments

We would like to thank the W.K. Kellogg Foundation and the Health Promotion Program at Michigan State University for providing the funding that enabled us to develop the curriculum on which this book is based. We would also like to thank the Psychology Department at Michigan State University for their support.

Thanks to our publisher, Judy Galbraith, for conceiving the idea of translating our concepts specifically for children. And thanks to our editor, Pamela Espeland, who labored with us to make this book possible.

CONTENTS

To Parents and Teachers vii

Introduction ix

    What It Means To Stick Up For Yourself x

    What You Need To Stick Up For Yourself......................xi

    How To Make This Book Work For You xii

GETTING AND USING PERSONAL POWER.....................1

Being Responsible..2

    Being Responsible For Your Behavior...............................3

    Being Responsible For Your Feelings................................6

Making Choices...8

    Expectations and Reality...10

Getting To Know Yourself..14

    Naming Your Feelings 15

    Growing a Feelings Vocabulary.......................................17

    Combination Feelings..30

    Talking About Feelings..31

    Naming Your Future Dreams..32

    Naming Your Needs...36

    How To Claim Your Feelings,
    Future Dreams, and Needs..44

    Talking Things Over With Yourself..................................46

    Great Escapes...48

Getting and Using Power in
Your Relationships and Your Life 51

    Two Kinds of Power..52

    Power In Your Relationships...54

    Power and Choice..55

    Equal Power 57

    Power In Your Life...59

How To Live Happily Ever After 61

  The Happiness List...62

LEARNING TO LIKE YOURSELF.......................................65

Listening To Your Inner Voices:
A Self-Esteem Self-Quiz 66

  The I-Did-It List...68

Self-Esteem Do's and Don'ts 70

Six Good Things To Do For Yourself 73

**Looking Back At The Beginning:
How Peter, Tara, and Sam
Can Stick Up For Themselves 75**

Index..77

About the Authors 81

TO PARENTS AND TEACHERS

Stick Up For Yourself! Every Kid's Guide to Personal Power and Positive Self-Esteem is based on a program originally developed for adults. The program, "Psychological Health and Self-Esteem," is currently offered as an undergraduate course in the Psychology Department at Michigan State University.

We believe that personal power and positive self-esteem are skills that can be learned. We further believe that all children should be taught these skills right along with reading, writing, and arithmetic.

It's our hope that the principles and tools presented here will one day be a regular part of the curriculum — that all kids will have the opportunity to learn how to stick up for themselves in healthy, meaningful ways. We have written this book to be used in the classroom and within the family. Please write to us and tell us how it works for you and the children in your charge. You may write to us at this address:

Gershen Kaufman and Lev Raphael
c/o Free Spirit Publishing Inc.
400 First Avenue North, Suite 616
Minneapolis, MN 55401

INTRODUCTION

Peter is having a bad day at school. The other kids are teasing him again. He tries to ignore them, but they just won't stop. Sometimes he feels like punching them all — or running away and not coming back.

That night he tells his mom about it. "I hate school," he says. "The kids all tease me. I wish I could quit."

"You know you can't quit school," his mom says. "What you need to do is stick up for yourself."

Tara's parents blame her for everything. Last night her little brother broke a plate, and they yelled at her! "If you had cleared the table like you were supposed to..." "If you had been watching him..." "If you would pay more attention..." Blah blah blah. It makes her sick!

Later Tara calls her best friend on the phone and tells her about it. "They blame me for stuff I don't even do," she says.

"Parents are really dense sometimes," her friend says. "What you have to do is stick up for yourself."

Sam's study hall teacher isn't fair. Sam knows the rule about not talking in study hall. He was doing his math, minding his own business, when Troy kicked him under the table. All Sam said was, "Hey! Cut it out!" Right away, the teacher orders him to stay after school! Sam tries to explain, but the teacher won't listen. And Troy sits there making faces!

He tells his family about it over dinner.

"You broke a rule," his dad says. "But it doesn't sound like you did it on purpose. You need to stick up for yourself."

Everyone tells you to stick up for yourself. But nobody tells you how. This book does.

What It Means To Stick Up For Yourself

When Peter's mom tells him to stick up for himself, what does that mean? Should he tease the other kids back? Should he get into fights? Should he tell the teacher?

When Tara's friend tells her to stick up for herself, what does that mean? Should she argue with her parents? Should she whack her little brother for getting her in trouble again? Should she go to her room and slam the door as loud as she can?

When Sam's father tells him to stick up for himself, what does that mean? Should Sam talk back to the teacher? Should he kick Troy and hope he talks, too? Should he go to the principal and complain about the teacher?

A lot of kids feel confused about what it means to stick up for yourself. So they do things it *doesn't* mean.

▶ Sticking up for yourself doesn't mean getting back at someone else.

▶ It doesn't mean acting bossy or stuck-up.

▶ It doesn't mean saying and doing whatever you want, whenever you want.

Here is what it does mean:

▶ Sticking up for yourself means being true to yourself.

▶ It means speaking up for yourself, when this is the right thing to do. (Sometimes it isn't.)

▶ It means there is always someone on your side — you!

What You Need To Stick Up For Yourself

There are things you need to make a painting: paints, a paintbrush, something to paint on. There are things you need to go running: feet, comfortable clothes, someplace to run.

There are things you need to stick up for yourself: *personal power* and *positive self-esteem.*

This book tells you how to get personal power. An important part of personal power is getting to know yourself. *You can't stick up for yourself if you don't know who you are.*

This book also tells you how to get positive self-esteem. *You can't stick up for yourself if you don't even like yourself.*

How To Make This Book Work For You

Do you know the story of *Alice in Wonderland?* Then maybe you remember "Drink Me" and "Eat Me." When Alice took a sip of Drink Me, she INSTANTLY got smaller! And when she took a bite of Eat Me, she INSTANTLY got bigger!

This book isn't anything like Drink Me or Eat Me. Reading it won't make you INSTANTLY able to stick up for yourself. Learning how takes time. It takes work. And it takes *wanting to change.*

We believe you can learn how to stick up for yourself. That is why we wrote this book for you. There are many ideas in it that aren't usually found in books for kids. But we believe kids can understand them and use them.

These tips can help you make this book work for you:

☞ Don't just read it. Do it! You will find many parts called "Getting Personal." Each one asks questions about you and your life. Try to answer the questions. You will learn a lot about yourself.

☞ Use a notebook or journal to write your "Getting Personal" answers. You can also use it to write down other thoughts you have when you're reading this book. You can write down stories from your own life that are like stories you read in this book.

☞ If you feel comfortable, share this book with an adult you trust and can talk to.

Finally, *let us know how this book works for you.* Write to us and tell us if it helps you stick up for yourself. Write to us and tell us if it doesn't. You can use this address:

Free Spirit Publishing Inc.
400 First Avenue North, Suite 616
Minneapolis, MN 55401

We really want to hear from you!

Best wishes,

Gershen Kaufman
and Lev Raphael
Spring 1990

GETTING AND USING PERSONAL POWER

WHAT DO YOU THINK when you hear the words "personal power"? Do you think they mean
(a) being stronger than everyone else?
(b) being smarter than everyone else?
(c) being able to make other people do what you want?
(d) having more money than other people?
(e) being famous, like a rock star, a movie star, or an athlete?

When we use the words "personal power," we don't mean any of those things. We think personal power means *being secure and confident inside yourself.*

That means anyone can have personal power. Even though you're "just a kid," you can have personal power. You can learn how to get it and how to use it. No matter how you feel inside yourself right now, you can learn to feel secure and confident.

It will take time and practice. It may take courage to make changes in your life. But you can do it!

Like the year has four seasons, personal power has four parts. They are:

1. **being responsible,**
2. **making choices,**
3. **getting to know yourself, and**
4. **getting and using power in your relationships and your life.**

BEING RESPONSIBLE

FACT:
You are responsible for
the kind of person you are
and how you live your life.

Maybe it doesn't seem that way to you. How can you be responsible if adults are always telling you what to do?

A lot of kids wonder about this. They confuse "being responsible" with "being in charge" or "being the boss" of other people and things.

• •
                          ▬▬▬▬▬▬▬▬▬

Becky is babysitting her little brother Robbie while their parents are visiting friends. Robbie wants to watch his favorite TV program. Becky wants to watch her favorite TV program. So Becky tells Robbie, "Mom and Dad said I was responsible. You have to do what I say." Becky is using "being responsible" as an excuse to get her way.

                          ▬▬▬▬▬▬▬▬▬
• •

There is something else that being responsible doesn't mean. It doesn't mean you have complete and final say over everything that happens to you.

There are many things you don't have any say over. Like the weather. Where your family lives. What school you go to. How much homework your teacher gives you. Whether someone decides to be your friend. And how other people act or feel.

You are responsible for *your own behavior* and y*our own feelings.*

Being Responsible For Your Behavior

• • • • • • • • • • • • • • ▬▬▬▬▬▬ • • • • • • • • • • • • • • •

Kevin and Jeff are playing race cars together on Kevin's track. Jeff's car keeps winning, and Kevin doesn't like that. It's his track! He should be winning! Suddenly Kevin reaches out and grabs Jeff's car and smashes it on the floor.

"Hey!" Jeff says. "What did you do that for?"

"I wouldn't have done it if you didn't keep winning," Kevin answers. "You made me do it."

▬▬▬▬▬▬

Trisha wants to go to her friend Lori's house to play.

"Have you finished picking up your room?" her mom wants to know.

"I'll do it later," Trisha promises.

"Please do it now," her mom says. "You can play with Lori when you're done."

Trisha gets really angry at her mom. She gets so angry that she throws her favorite toy across the room. It breaks! Tearfully, she gathers up the pieces and takes them to her mom. "Look what you made me do!" she sobs.

▬▬▬▬▬▬
• • • • • • • • • • • • • • • ▬▬▬▬▬▬ • • • • • • • • • • • • • •

Sometimes other people do or say things we don't like. Maybe we get angry or frustrated. We may want to do something to get back at them. And we may feel that what we do is their fault.

We are responsible for only our own behavior. Jeff didn't "make" Kevin smash his car. Trisha's mom didn't "make" Trisha break her favorite toy. Kevin and Trisha need to take responsibility for their own behavior.

• •
▬▬▬▬▬▬▬▬▬▬▬

Max and Zachary are not supposed to go to the store by themselves. Their parents think they are too young and have told them not to go.

One day Zachary talks Max into going to the store with him to buy some candy. "Don't be a baby, Mom and Dad will never find out," Zachary says.

Well, their parents do find out. "Why did you go when you know you're not supposed to?" they ask the boys.

"It was Zachary's idea," Max says. "He made me do it."

▬▬▬▬▬▬▬▬▬▬▬
• •

Sometimes we let other people talk us into doing things we know we shouldn't. We think this makes us not responsible for what we do. But Zachary didn't "make" Max disobey their parents and go to the store. Max needs to take responsibility for his own behavior.

• •
▬▬▬▬▬▬▬▬▬▬▬

"Mo-om!" Tiffany shouts. "Robin ate the last cookie!"

"You were supposed to save that for Tiffany," their mom scolds Robin.

"But I didn't mean to eat it!" Robin answers.

▬▬▬▬▬▬▬▬▬▬▬
• •

Sometimes we do things just because we feel like it. We don't think about what will happen next or how someone else might feel. But saying "we didn't mean it" doesn't undo what we did. Robin needs to take responsibility for her own behavior.

Kids aren't the only ones who get mixed up about this. There are plenty of adults who don't take responsibility for their behavior. Maybe you've heard some adults say things like, "I'm sorry I spanked you. But you make me so angry that I can't help myself!" Or "If I'm grumpy, it's your fault for arguing with me."

Or "I didn't mean to miss your birthday party. I had to go to a meeting after work."

Adults may use more and bigger words than kids, but what they're saying is just the same: "I'm not responsible!" Now you know this isn't true. So the next time an adult says, "You made me do it!" you can tell yourself, "I didn't make that person do anything. I'm responsible only for my own behavior." *This is a way to stick up for yourself.*

When we know — *really know* — that we are responsible for our own behavior, we can make some important decisions for ourselves.

▶ We can decide to tell the truth and not exaggerate or make things up.

▶ We can decide to be the kind of person other people can count on.

▶ We can decide to keep our hands to ourselves even when we get mad and feel like hitting someone.

▶ We can decide to do our school work and our chores without being nagged or reminded.

Being responsible usually makes good things happen at home and in school. The more responsible we are, the more people trust us, and the more privileges we get.

But this isn't the main reason to start being responsible. The main reason is because it's the best thing to do for you. It helps you feel secure and confident inside yourself. It gives you a feeling of personal power.

Here's something else you should know: *Being responsible* isn't the same as *being perfect.* You'll still make mistakes. You'll still do things you're not supposed to do. So what? Everybody does. Nobody's perfect!

Being Responsible For Your Feelings

Someone else can't "make" you smash another person's car, break your favorite toy, or disobey your parents. In the same way, no one can "make" you happy or unhappy, excited or angry, bored or curious, or any other feeling. *You are responsible for your own feelings.*

Sometimes things other people say or do can act as "triggers" for our feelings.

• • • • • • • • • • • • • • • • • • ▬▬▬▬▬▬ • • • • • • • • • • • • • • • • • •

"Did you put your bike away when you got home from school?" David's dad asks him.

"Not yet," David answers absent-mindedly. He is busy putting landing wheels on his model airplane.

"You never do it when you're supposed to!" his dad yells. "I want you to do it now!"

Suddenly David feels hurt and angry. His dad is so mean and unfair! Why does he have to yell? It seems like he always yells! He always accuses David of not doing his chores on time! His dad's words and yelling trigger David's hurt, angry feelings.

• • • • • • • • • • • • • • • • • • ▬▬▬▬▬▬ • • • • • • • • • • • • • • • • • •

But maybe David often has to be reminded to do his chores. Maybe he's in the habit of doing other things first or instead. So when he says "not yet," this triggers frustrated, angry feelings in his dad.

We can learn to ignore triggers and decide for ourselves how we want to feel.

MAKING CHOICES

FACT:

Because you are responsible

for your behavior and feelings,

you can make choices about them.

You can choose how to act. You can choose not to smash a friend's car or break a toy or disobey your parents. Even if you feel like doing these things. Even if the feeling seems overpowering or irresistible.

Many times, our actions are tied to our feelings. We hit someone because we feel angry. We kick the wall because we feel frustrated. We cry because we feel sad.

You can choose how angry, frustrated, or sad to feel. You can even choose to have different feelings.

• •
▬▬▬▬▬▬▬▬

Sara studied hard for her spelling test. But when the test came, she still got six wrong. Her teacher wrote across the top, in big red letters, "You can do better!"

▬▬▬▬▬▬▬▬
• •

Sara has many choices about how to feel. She can feel angry at her teacher for not seeing how hard she studied. She can feel angry at herself for not doing better on the test. She can think, "If I were smarter I wouldn't get so many wrong. I must be pretty stupid." OR she can tell herself, "I did the best I could on this test, and what I did is *good enough!*"

• •
▬▬▬▬▬▬▬▬

Larry comes home from school excited to tell his mom about his day. His team won at volley-ball...he had a fun band lesson...he finished his homework in study period...everything went great! But when he rushes in the door, his mom is on the telephone. She signals him to be quiet until she's through talking.

▬▬▬▬▬▬▬▬
• •

Larry has choices about how to feel. He can feel rejected. He can think, "If I was more important than that person on the telephone, my mom would hang up right away and pay attention to me." OR he can tell himself, "She probably won't be on the phone for very long. I can wait. I can read a book while I wait so the time will go faster."

● ●

Carlos loves his cat. He raised it from the time it was a kitten. It sleeps in his bed at night and walks with him to the school bus every day.

But one day the cat gets very sick. Carlos's dad takes it to the pet doctor. The pet doctor does not think the cat will ever get well. He thinks the cat might die.

● ●

It is normal and natural to feel sadness and grief at times like these. When someone or something we love seems about to die or be taken away from us, we can feel lonely and scared.

Still, Carlos has choices. He can choose to feel sad and worried all alone. OR he can choose to share his feelings with his dad. Together they can talk about Carlos's cat and why it means so much to him. This might not make Carlos feel happy, but he will probably feel less sad and worried. It helps to have someone listen to us and understand our feelings.

You can choose how to handle what life hands you. You can choose how you will face life's problems. This sounds like a lot for someone who is "just a kid." But we believe that everyone can learn to do it.

Expectations and Reality

An important part of learning to make choices is learning to make wise choices. This starts with deciding what we expect to happen as a result of our choice, and whether our expectations are *realistic*.

In other words: What do we hope will happen because of our choice? What are the chances it will happen? If the chances are good, then our choice is realistic. If the chances are terrible, then our choice is not realistic.

• •
━━━━━━━━━

Christopher has signed up to play basketball in after-school sports. He plans to practice every day and not miss a single game. He expects that by the end of the year he will be the very best basketball player in the school — maybe even the whole league!

━━━━━━━━━
• •

It's great that Christopher wants to play basketball. It's great that he plans to practice and go to all the games. But when Christopher expects that he will be the *very best* basketball player, he is not being realistic.

Maybe he will be a good basketball player. Maybe he will even be an excellent basketball player. It depends on how hard he practices and if he has a talent for basketball. But will he be the *very best* basketball player? The chances are not very good. There can be only one *very best*, and there are many other kids in the league.

We live in a culture that values success almost more than anything else. It is important in our culture to be the best, the strongest, the fastest, the richest, the most popular, the biggest star. But that's not what personal power means. It means *doing our personal best at the things we believe are important.* And it means *liking ourselves even if our best isn't THE best.*

What are some realistic expectations Christopher can have instead? He can expect to learn a lot about basketball. He can expect to get better at dribbling, shooting baskets, and playing different positions. He can expect that *it will take time* to learn these new skills. He can expect to have fun learning and playing. He can expect to make new friends on the team. Most important, he can expect to make mistakes instead of thinking he has to be perfect! These are all realistic expectations.

• •

Tai's family has just moved to a new town, and this is Tai's first day at her new school. At first she feels nervous and afraid. What if the other kids don't like her? What if she gets lost or does something dumb? What if she doesn't fit in?

By the end of the day, she feels much better. Another girl named Shelley has been friendly to her all day. Shelley showed her where the lunchroom was and where to buy milk. She invited her to play with her at recess.

That night, over dinner, Tai tells her family about her day. "I really like my new school!" she says. "This girl Shelley was really nice to me. I think she's going to be my best friend!"

• •

It's great that Tai feels excited about her new school. It's great that she wants to be friends with Shelley. But when Tai expects Shelley to be her best friend, she is not being realistic.

Maybe Shelley already has a best friend. Maybe Tai and Shelley don't have that much in common after all. Or maybe they do, and they will turn out to be good friends. Who knows? Right now is too soon to decide.

Almost everyone has a hard time being realistic about relationships. This includes adults. We expect people to care about us just because we care about them. We forget that we can't control how they behave and how they feel.

What are some realistic expectations Tai can have instead? She can expect to make friends at her new school. If she is a friendly person, then other kids will probably want to be friends with her. She can expect that *it will take time* to decide which kids *she* likes and respects. She can also expect that *it will take time* for them to decide if they like and respect her. Maybe one or more of them will want to be close friends with her — even best friends! These are all realistic expectations.

GETTING TO KNOW YOURSELF

• •

Jennifer works hard to fit in with the popular group at school. She likes the same things they like. She hates the same things they hate. She bugs her parents to buy her the same clothes. She spends her allowance on the same music. She wears her hair the same way. She uses the same slang words. And on and on! It's hard to keep up. Sometimes Jennifer wishes she could just be herself.

Marcus really wants to play soccer. He likes watching soccer games on TV. Over and over, he imagines himself actually becoming a soccer player. He feels very excited about it, and he thinks he would be good at soccer. Becoming a soccer player is a future dream for Marcus.

But when sports sign-up time comes, his dad has big news. "I'm going to coach a softball team this year," his dad says. "You'll be on my team. We'll have a great time together!"

Marcus doesn't know whether to do what he wants, or what his dad wants. Finally he decides to go along with his dad. He plays softball instead of soccer.

• •

Maybe you know people like Jennifer and Marcus. Maybe you're thinking, "They should stick up for themselves!" And you're right.

If you work too hard to please other people, it's hard to get to know yourself. And this makes it hard to stick up for yourself. But you can make a change. A good place to start is by *naming and claiming* your feelings, future dreams, and needs.

Naming Your Feelings

Back when you were learning to talk, you only knew a few words and sounds you thought were words. So you had to use one word or sound to name many things.

Maybe you said "wah-wah" when you meant water — and milk, and juice, and all of the other things you liked to drink. When you said "wah-wah" to your mom, she had to guess what you really wanted!

Later, as you learned more words, you could be more specific. You could say "milk" when you wanted milk, "juice" when you wanted juice. From there you learned to say "apple juice" and "orange juice." You made an important discovery: The more *names* of things you knew, the more you could ask for what you really wanted!

Feelings have their own special names. The more names you know, the more you can understand your feelings and tell other people about them. And the more you can stick up for yourself.

Names are like "handles" for our feelings. Knowing the right name for a feeling allows us to "pick it up," learn about it, and make choices about it.

Calling feelings by their right names adds to your personal power. Calling feelings by their wrong names takes away from your personal power.

• •
■■■■■■■■■■■■■

Tracy is lying on her bed with her pillow over her head. She just had a terrible day at school. Her best friend acted mean to her. Her teacher scolded her for not paying attention.

Tracy's dad comes into her room and sees her lying there. "Is something wrong?" he asks. "Do you want to talk about it?"

"No," Tracy sighs. "I'm too depressed right now."

"That's silly," her dad answers. "Ten-year-olds don't get depressed. You're probably just tired."

■■■■■■■■■■■■■
• •

If Tracy goes along with what her dad tells her, she may learn to call her feeling by the wrong name. Whenever she feels depressed, she'll think or say, "I'm tired." She'll lose the "handle" for her feeling.

• •
■■■■■■■■■■■■■

Jerome is having a problem about his sister, May. It seems like his mom is always *thinking of her first! May has to go to skating lessons. May is in the school play. May gets straight A's. May gets all the attention!*

His mom can tell there's something wrong with Jerome. "What's the matter with you lately?" she asks him one day.

"It seems like the only person you care about is May," he says. "I guess I feel jealous."

"It's not nice to be jealous," his mom says. "Jealousy is a bad feeling."

■■■■■■■■■■■■■
• •

If Jerome goes along with what his mom tells him, he may learn to feel ashamed of his jealousy. He may even begin to deny his jealousy or lock it out of his mind.

Feelings aren't "wrong" or "right," "bad" or "good." *Feelings just are.* Understanding this makes it possible for you to claim all of your feelings. If you think you feel depressed, then that's the way you feel. If you think you feel jealous, then that's the way you feel. Nobody can "make" you feel a different way. Nobody knows more about your feelings than you do.

Growing a Feelings Vocabulary

How good are you at naming your feelings? Is it easy or hard for you to come up with the right words to describe how you feel?

You can grow a "feelings vocabulary" by listening to other people talk about their feelings, by asking for help explaining your own feelings, and by reading about feelings, the way you are doing now.

Dr. Silvan Tomkins is a psychologist who has spent a long time studying people's feelings. He believes that most feelings can be grouped into eight basic types. Each type includes a *low-intensity feeling* and a *high-intensity feeling*. The high-intensity feeling is stronger.

Here are the eight basic types of feelings Dr. Tomkins has named:

Low-Intensity	*High-Intensity*
1. Interested	Excited
2. Enjoying Yourself	Joyful
3. Surprised	Startled
4. Distressed	Anguished
5. Fearful	Terrified
6. Angry	Enraged
7. Ashamed	Humiliated
8. Contemptuous	Disgusted

Interested

When you're *interested* in something, you're curious about it, paying attention to it, even concentrating on it. Things you might be interested in are:

- ▶ a good book
- ▶ a conversation you're overhearing
- ▶ a video game
- ▶ a TV program
- ▶ learning something new in school

GETTING PERSONAL
Name at least five things you're
interested in.

More names for interested: curious, fascinated, intrigued
Opposites: bored, uncaring

Excited

When you're *excited* about something, you may not be able to think about anything else! Things you might be excited about are:

- ▶ going on vacation
- ▶ making a new friend
- ▶ your birthday
- ▶ finding the final baseball card you need to complete your collection

---

GETTING PERSONAL
Name at least five things you
get excited about.

More names for excited: thrilled, eager, happy
Opposites: sleepy, dull, blah, bored

Enjoying Yourself

When you're *enjoying yourself,* you're smiling and feeling good.
Times you might be enjoying yourself are when:

▶   you're playing quietly with a friend
▶   your mother is reading you to sleep
▶   you're petting a cat or dog
▶   you're relaxing with your favorite hobby

GETTING PERSONAL
Name at least five things you
enjoy doing.

More names for enjoying yourself: pleased, relaxed, satisfied,
contented
Opposites: unhappy, tense, exhausted

Joyful

When you're *joyful,* it's as if your whole body is full of happiness. You feel bubbly inside. The world seems like a wonderful place. Times you might be joyful are when:

▶ it's your birthday and you get all the presents you hoped for

▶ you win first place in the chess tournament

▶ you fly on an airplane to visit your grandparents

▶ somebody you like a lot finally notices you

GETTING PERSONAL
Write about a time when you
felt joyful.

More names for joyful: glad, ecstatic, walking on air, flying high, joyous
Opposites: unhappy, "down," depressed, sad, lonely

Surprised

When you're *surprised* by something, you may not know how to act at first. To be surprised is to experience something you weren't expecting. Things that might surprise you are:

▶ getting a letter from a friend who moved away a long time ago

▶ learning that your teacher went to school with your mom

▶ the first snowfall of the season

▶ receiving an unexpected gift

▶ a compliment

GETTING PERSONAL
Write about a time when you
felt surprised.

More names for surprised: amazed, astonished, impressed
Opposites: bored, blasé, indifferent, ho-hum

Startled

When you're *startled* by something — like a sudden CRASH nearby — your first response is shock. Things that might startle you are:

- ▶ someone jumps out at you from behind a tree
- ▶ you step off a curb into a puddle of icy water
- ▶ you sit down on a chair and find out — too late! — that it doesn't have a bottom
- ▶ a dog barks suddenly right behind you

GETTING PERSONAL
Write about a time when you
felt startled.

More names for startled: jolted, shocked, alarmed
Opposites: calm, settled, reassured, peaceful

Distressed

When you're *distressed* about something, you feel sad about it, and sometimes you cry. Things that might distress you are:

▶   hearing your parents argue
▶   when your best friend moves away
▶   finding out that someone you love is sick
▶   being punished unfairly

GETTING PERSONAL
Write about a time when you
felt distressed.

More names for distressed: upset, sad, tearful, crying, sobbing
Opposites: relieved, comforted, cheerful

Anguished

When you're *anguished* about something, you're in *very great* distress. Other words for "anguish" are "agony," "misery," "suffering," and "despair." This is a strong and painful feeling! Things you might feel anguished about are:

▶   the death of someone you love
▶   knowing that something you did has hurt another person very badly
▶   believing that you've just lost your best friend
▶   a divorce in your family

GETTING PERSONAL
Write about a time when you have
felt anguished. Tell what happened
and what you did.
Have you ever told anyone else
about this? Think about telling an
adult — someone you trust and can
talk to.

More names for anguished: suffering, tormented, grieving, tortured

Opposites: reassured, safe, soothed

Fearful

When you are *fearful,* you're worried and afraid. You think that something is about to happen, or someone is about to say something, to threaten you. Things that can make you fearful are:

▶   being all alone in the house
▶   your first day at a new school
▶   thinking about tomorrow's math test
▶   hearing that a big storm is coming
▶   being bullied or threatened by someone

GETTING PERSONAL
Name at least five things that make
you fearful.

More names for fearful: scared, frightened, worried, nervous

Opposites: confident, brave, fearless, trusting, hopeful

Terrified

When you're *terrified,* you're *very* frightened. You may feel paralyzed with fear — as if you can't move, even to help yourself. Things that can terrify you are:

- ▶ a really bad nightmare
- ▶ getting lost or separated from your family in a strange place
- ▶ being in a car that's about to crash
- ▶ being in a disaster, like a hurricane or an earthquake

GETTING PERSONAL

Write about a time when you felt terrified. Tell what happened and what you did.

More names for terrified: frightened, petrified, in a panic
Opposites: relaxed, encouraged, courageous

Angry

Anger can be sudden and fierce, here and gone in a flash. Or it can start slowly and build, then burn for a long time. You might feel angry at a particular person or about a particular thing. Or you might feel angry at everybody and everything.

Some people confuse feeling angry with feeling powerful. Because anger is such a strong feeling, they think that anger makes them strong. Remember that personal power means being secure and confident inside yourself.

Times you might feel angry are when:

- ▶ your sister reads your diary without asking
- ▶ a teacher says you were cheating when you weren't
- ▶ a friend breaks a promise to you
- ▶ your parents ground you for breaking a rule

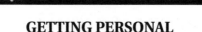

GETTING PERSONAL
Write about a time when you felt
angry. Tell what happened and what
you did.

More names for angry: mad, bitter, irritated, indignant, resentful
Opposites: loving, friendly, peaceful, agreeable

Enraged

Rage is anger that boils over and blows up. Or it stays hidden inside, waiting to boil up and blow over, like a volcano. To feel *enraged* is to feel out of control. Times you might feel enraged are when:

▶ someone shames you or humiliates you by insulting you, beating you up, or making fun of you

▶ someone takes something that belongs to you and won't give it back

▶ someone spreads lies about you and everyone else believes them

▶ your parents change the rules and you feel powerless

GETTING PERSONAL
Write about a time when you felt
enraged. Tell what happened and
what you did.

More names for enraged: furious, boiling, "seeing red"
Opposites: calm, quiet, soothed

Ashamed

When you're *ashamed,* you feel exposed. You want to run and hide or cover yourself up. It feels like everyone suddenly "knows" you're just no good. Something is wrong with you inside and everyone can see it! Times you might feel ashamed are when:

- ▶ you ask someone for help and that person says, "Go away, don't bother me"
- ▶ your parents scold you for crying, saying, "Stop being a baby!"
- ▶ you have to give a speech in front of your class and suddenly your mind goes blank
- ▶ you want to approach someone you don't know, but you feel tongue-tied
- ▶ you trip or fall and everyone around laughs at you

GETTING PERSONAL
Write about a time when you felt ashamed. Tell what happened and what you did.
Have you ever told anyone else about this? Think about telling an adult — someone you trust and can talk to.

More names for ashamed: exposed, discouraged, uncomfortable, embarrassed, shy, guilty, self-conscious
Opposites: confident, proud, "on top of the world"

Humiliated

When you're *humiliated,* you're deeply and publicly ashamed. You feel completely defeated by someone or something. You wonder if you can ever show your face again! Times you might feel humiliated are when:

- ▶ you forget your lines in the school play on opening night
- ▶ a parent scolds you in front of your friends
- ▶ another kid beats you up at school
- ▶ someone you trusted reveals a secret about you to other people
- ▶ the kids at school start calling you a really terrible nickname

GETTING PERSONAL

Write about a time when you felt humiliated. Tell what happened and what you did.
Have you ever told anyone else about this? Think about telling an adult — someone you trust and can talk to.

More names for humiliated: mortified, disgraced, defeated, alienated
Opposites: proud, elated

Contemptuous

To feel *contemptuous* is to look down on other people. You think you're better than they are. You feel as if there's "something wrong" with them, and they don't deserve to be liked or respected.

Sometimes contempt is a defense, a way to protect yourself against painful or uncomfortable feelings. For kids who feel left out, who think they don't "fit in," being contemptuous is a way to feel "above it all" and prove that "it doesn't matter."

Times you might feel contemptuous are when:

▶   the other kids seem slower or not as smart as you, and you feel superior to them

▶   you're lonely and you don't know how to start making friends, so you decide you "don't care" or you "don't need anyone"

▶   other kids don't let you join their club, so you decide the club is "stupid" and not worth joining

▶   you're afraid to try something new but you don't want to show it, so instead you act "above it all"

▶   someone has insulted you and you want to put that person down

GETTING PERSONAL

Write about a time when you felt contempt for another person. Tell what happened and what you did.

More names for contemptuous: scornful, disrespectful, stuck-up, smug, snooty, sarcastic
Opposites: humble, respectful, admiring

Disgusted

When you're *disgusted* with someone, you can hardly stand to be around that person. You feel as if that person "makes you sick." You feel like getting rid of that person, the way you would spit something out. It's also possible to feel disgusted with yourself.

Times you might feel disgusted are when:

▶ you discover that a good friend has lied to you

▶ you realize that your parents aren't perfect

▶ you feel too grown-up for "little kid" stuff

▶ you stop liking someone and you don't want to be around that person anymore

---

GETTING PERSONAL

Write about a time when you felt disgusted with another person. Tell what happened and what you did. Then write about a time when you felt disgusted with yourself.

More names for disgusted: revolted, repelled, put off by

Opposites: affectionate, impressed, fond of

Combination Feelings

Maybe you used to think that being "surprised" and being "startled" were the same. Or that being "fearful" and being "terrified" were the same.

Now you know they are different. You know that each feeling has its own special name. You're growing a "feelings vocabulary" and getting to know yourself better.

Sometimes it can be hard to tell feelings apart. That's because you can have more than one feeling at a time. Or you can have many feelings in a row, coming so quickly they seem to mix together. We call these "combination feelings."

▶ For example, you might feel *startled* first, then *angry* right after. Like the time when someone jumped out at you and really scared you. You wanted to punch that person!

▶ You might be *enjoying yourself* when somebody says something rude to you, and all at once you feel *humiliated*. For example, you're looking through a box of toys when you discover your old blocks. You take them out and build a tower — it's fun! Then your big sister comes into your room and says, "Look at the little baby playing with blocks!"

▶ You might go from being *surprised* to being *joyful*. Like the time your parents threw a surprise birthday party for you, or bought you a present you weren't expecting.

▶ You might go from feeling *ashamed* to feeling *enraged*. Shame and rage are very closely connected. Rage is a way to "cover up" shame so it doesn't show as much.

Just as the primary colors — red, yellow, and blue — can be mixed to make more colors, the eight basic types of feelings can be mixed to make more feelings.

Talking About Feelings

Talking about feelings should be a regular part of life. Unfortunately, for many people, it isn't. They're uncomfortable talking about their own feelings. They're uncomfortable listening to other people talk about feelings. Maybe some of the adults in your life are like this.

Try to find someone you can talk to about your feelings. Start with your parents. Try a teacher or the school counselor, your minister or rabbi. Maybe a brother or a sister. You *will* find someone who speaks your language! You *will* find someone who listens and wants to understand.

Try to remember that feelings aren't "wrong" or "right," "bad" or "good." *Feelings just are.* All of your feelings are okay for you to have because they're *your* feelings. No one can take them away from you unless you let them. No one can make you change your feelings unless you let them. So don't! Claim your feelings as your own.

Naming Your Future Dreams

For this part of the book, you will need three things:

1. your memory,
2. your eyes, and
3. your imagination.

Try to have these three things, too:

1. a photograph of yourself at age 5 that shows your face and eyes,
2. a mirror, and
3. a time machine.

You probably don't have a *real* time machine, so you'll have to imagine one. Maybe you can imagine one that's just the right size to slip over the chair you're sitting in now.

1. Using your memory, your photograph, and your time machine, go back in time to when you were five years old.

What kind of person were you? What things were important to you? What dreams did you have for yourself?

GETTING PERSONAL

Write about yourself as a
five-year-old. It might help to write as
if you were describing someone else.
For example, "Sharon is in kinder-
garten. She likes to dance and play
with her dog, Toby. She wants to be
an astronaut when she grows up…"

---

2. Using your eyes and your mirror, look at the person you are today.

How have you changed? What things are important to you now? What people are important to you? Are you happy? Do you like yourself? Are you doing some things you want to do, things that matter to you? What are your personal goals? What are you "living for"? What are your dreams for yourself? What are some things you would like to change about yourself and your life?

GETTING PERSONAL

Write about the person you
are today.

---

3. Using your imagination and your time machine, go forward in time to your future.

What are you doing? What kind of life are you living? What is your job or career? Where are you living? Are you married? Do you have children? What have been your most important achievements? What are you most proud of? Have you met your personal goals? Have you made your dreams come true? What do you want to do next?

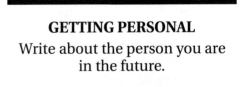

GETTING PERSONAL
Write about the person you are
in the future.

Writing about who you might be someday is a way to start thinking about your future dreams. Your future dreams are your personal goals. They give your life direction, purpose, and meaning. They guide your decisions and help you define the kind of person you are and want to be.

Your dreams can be for the near future or the far future. Examples of dreams for the near future are:

— "to make friends at school with kids I respect"
— "to compliment at least one person every day when I mean it"
— "to be healthy"
— "to learn as much as I can about photography"
— "to read more and watch less TV"
— "to earn three more merit badges in Scouts"

Examples of dreams for the far future are:

— "to become a professional basketball player"
— "to become a dancer"
— "to become a scientist"
— "to someday have children of my own"
— "to get a job where I can work with animals"

GETTING PERSONAL

Make a list of your Top 10 future dreams. Which ones are for the near future? Which ones are for the far future?
Put your list away for a few weeks, then look at it again. Has anything changed?

You may wonder where your future dreams come from. You aren't born with them. You can't buy them at a store. In fact, they come from many different people and places. Some of these are:

▶ your parents
▶ your teachers
▶ other people you look up to or admire

▶   your religious leaders
▶   your friends
▶   your peer group (people your age)
▶   the music you listen to
▶   what you read in books, magazines, and newspapers
▶   TV shows and movies
▶   your imagination

Here is something else you should know about future dreams: *They change.* Yours won't stay the same for your whole life. As things change around you — as *you* change inside — you'll need to keep deciding what you want to be and do.

Naming Your Needs

"Need" is a word we all use a lot. We talk about "needing" to see a new movie, or "needing" a new engine for our train set, or "needing" to get a haircut or a pro jacket.

But these aren't needs. These are *wants.* Needs and wants aren't the same.

There are seven basic needs that all people share:

1. the need for relationships with other people
2. the need for touching and holding
3. the need to belong and feel "one" with others
4. the need to be different and separate
5. the need to nurture (to care for and help other people)
6. the need to feel worthwhile, valued, and admired
7. the need for power in our relationships and our lives

Like feelings, needs aren't right or wrong, good or bad. *Needs just are.* The more you know about your needs, the more you can understand them and tell other people about them. And the more you can stick up for yourself.

The Need for Relationships with Other People

From the moment we're born, we need to care about other people. We need them to care about us. We need to feel *absolutely, positively sure* that we're important and wanted. We need to feel special in each of our relationships.

As you grow up and get older, some people may tell you, "It's not good to need or depend on other people. It's better to stand on your own two feet." We live in a culture that values independence. Our culture says that only weak people need other people.

In fact, it takes real strength to have relationships with people. Sometimes it's hard to be friends. Sometimes it's hard to be a sister or brother. Later in life you'll find out that sometimes it's hard to be married, and sometimes it's hard to be a parent.

If you need other people, if you have relationships with other people, then you aren't weak! *You're strong.* Needing is a source of strength.

GETTING PERSONAL

Write about your most important relationships. Who are the people you care about most, who care the most about you? Ask one of your important people for some "special time" together. (When you do this, you are asking to have your need met.) Later, write about how you felt and how the other person acted.

The Need for Touching and Holding

Babies, kids, teenagers, grownups, grandmas and grandpas — *everyone* needs to be touched and held sometimes.

Touching and holding are ways we show affection for one another. When your mom hugs you or kisses you good-bye when you leave for school, this says, "I love you a lot."

Touching and holding are ways we comfort one another. When you fall off your bike and run to your dad and he hugs you, this says, "I am here to help you feel better."

Scientists know that babies need to be touched and held. When babies don't get enough touching and holding, they don't develop properly. They have physical and mental problems. Our need to be touched and held doesn't go away as we get older. We never outgrow it.

Unfortunately, we live in a culture that confuses touching and holding with sex. That is why, as you get older, you may get mixed messages about touching and holding. Friends who touch each other will get teased and called names. Parents may suddenly decide that their teenage sons and daughters are "too old" to be hugged and kissed. This is a problem with our culture. It isn't a problem with you. It's still okay to need touching and holding.

Of course, you should never let anyone touch you in ways that feel bad to you. Remember, there's *good touch* and there's *bad touch*. Your parents and teachers have probably told you the difference. If they haven't, ask an adult you trust to explain it to you.

GETTING PERSONAL

Ask someone you trust for a hug.
Write about what happens and how
you feel.

The Need To Belong and Feel "One" With Others

Tomas wants to grow up to be just like his dad. Emily wants to grow up to be just like her mother. Josh looks up to his older brother. Kelly hopes that someday she will be as smart as her teacher. And Tim can't stop talking about his hero, a baseball player.

From an early age, we all have people we look up to and admire. And we want to be like them. We may copy the way they walk or dress and the things they say. This helps us feel like we are part of their lives, even part of them on the inside. We feel like we belong. We feel like we are "one" with them.

Another way we meet our need to feel "one" with others is by joining groups. Scouts, sports teams, computer club, and our church or temple are all examples of groups we can join.

GETTING PERSONAL

Name five people you look up to and admire. Who do you most want to be like? Why?

Name the groups or organizations you belong to. Tell what you like best about each one.

The Need To Be Different and Separate

We all need to feel different, unique, and separate. We need to be able to say to ourselves, "There is nobody else like me in the whole world."

We also need to be able to say to others, "I'm *not* you, I'm different from you." We may even need to say "no" to things they have taught us. This is how we define and discover who we really are and what we really believe.

The need to feel different and separate may seem like the opposite of the need to belong and feel "one" with others. In fact, it is. You will go back-and-forth between these two needs throughout your life. Sometimes you'll copy other people you admire. Sometimes you'll let your own talents, interests, and abilities come out.

GETTING PERSONAL

Describe five ways you're different
from the people in your family.
Describe five ways you're different
from your friends. Be proud of
these differences.

The Need To Nurture

Aleisha waits for her dad to take a nap. Then she quietly opens the door, goes outside, and starts washing the car.

Aleisha feels excited. Her dad doesn't know she is washing the car. It will be a big surprise! She thinks about what will happen when her dad wakes up. He'll come outside and see a clean, shiny car. Aleisha knows that her dad will be happy. The whole time she works on the car, she feels good inside.

Darryl looks at the clock on the classroom wall. Only four more hours until the school roller-skating party! Everyone's going — kids, parents, teachers, even the principal.

"I'll be there," his teacher is saying. "But I'm not a very good skater. I just hope nobody laughs at me!" She smiles to let the class know that she doesn't mind not being a good skater.

That night, at the roller-skating rink, Darryl sees his teacher. She is skating very slowly next to the rail. Darryl skates over to her. "Here," he says, "you can take my arm. I'll help you skate around the rink."

"Why, thank you, Darryl!" his teacher exclaims. "This is really thoughtful of you."

Darryl grins. He feels good inside.

We all need to nurture other people. We need to help them and show that we care about them.

Nurturing other people makes them feel good. It also makes us feel good inside.

GETTING PERSONAL

Describe five times when you have helped other people. Tell how you felt and how they acted.

The Need To Feel Worthwhile, Valued, and Admired

Have you ever asked your mom, dad, or others to watch you do something — like play an instrument, dance, or shoot baskets? Do you remember the look in their eyes when they watched you?

We all need to feel worthwhile and valued. We need to feel recognized and openly admired.

At first we count on other people to help us feel this way. In time we learn to encourage and praise ourselves. Think of a baby who is just starting to walk. At first she counts on her parents to help her stand up, lead her by the hand, and pick her up when she falls. In time she learns to walk by herself.

When someone we care about says, "You're a good speller," we start to think, "I'm a good speller." When someone we care about says, "I like the way you talk to your little sister," we start to think, "I'm a kind person." As other people notice our talents and abilities, we feel more secure about them. We start to *know* that we are worthwhile and valued and *deserve* to be admired.

GETTING PERSONAL

Name at least five of your talents and abilities. Now name at least five people who help you feel worthwhile, valued, and admired.

The Need for Power in Our Relationships and Our Lives

So far we've been talking about personal power — being secure and confident inside yourself. But there's another kind of power we all need.

We need to feel that we have power in our relationships with other people. (This is not the same as having power *over* people.) And we need to feel that we're in charge of our own lives.

Whenever you can make choices about things like what or when to eat, what to wear, bedtimes, or music lessons, you're exercising power. There are many things you don't have power over. But there are some things you do have power over.

GETTING PERSONAL

Name five things you have power
over at home. Then name five
things you *don't* have power over
at home.
Pick one thing you *don't* have power
over. Talk about it with your mom or
dad. Work together to come up with
two choices you can have about it.

Later we'll tell you ways to get and use power in your
relationships and your life. But first there's something else you
should know about your feelings, future dreams, and needs.

How To Claim Your Feelings, Future Dreams, and Needs

*Mario can't find one of his winter gloves. He
thinks he left it on the playground at recess. He
knows there's a Lost-and-Found box in the school
office. So he goes to the office after school and asks
to see the Lost-and-Found box.*

*"I'm looking for my glove," he tells the school
secretary. "It's blue with Batman on it." And there
it is, sitting right on top of the box. "I found it!" he
says. "This is my glove."*

Mario *names* his glove. He doesn't say, "I'm looking for a mitten," or "I'm looking for a striped scarf." Then he *claims* his glove. He doesn't say, "This is my glove, but what is it doing here?" He doesn't say, "This is my glove, but it sure is ugly." He doesn't question or judge it. He simply accepts it. The glove belongs to him.

This is the way to claim your feelings, future dreams, and needs. Don't question or judge them. Simply *experience them, name them*, and *accept them*. They belong to you.

Why should you care about claiming your feelings, future dreams, and needs? Because naming them isn't enough to make them yours. What if Mario had said, "This is my glove," and then left it in the Lost-and-Found box? He would have known where to find his glove. But he wouldn't have been able to use it.

It is important to use *all* of your feelings, future dreams, and needs. Not just the ones that seem easy and safe. Not just the ones other people say you should use.

▶ Maybe you don't like feeling ashamed. You wish you could leave that feeling in a Lost-and-Found box!

▶ Or maybe one of your future dreams is turning out to be a pain. You really want to learn to play the trumpet. But learning means practicing, and practicing takes time!

▶ Or maybe you're having a problem with your need for touching and holding. It's embarrassing when your mom hugs you. Especially in front of your friends. Yet you like it when she hugs you, and you miss it when she doesn't....Aaarrggh! How confusing!

You may try to push away some feelings, future dreams, and needs, or lock them up inside yourself. This isn't a good idea, because they don't stay away or locked up. They can turn into big problems later.

Many adults today have big problems in their lives. Doctors think it's because they pushed away or locked up important feelings, future dreams, and needs when they were kids. When we do this, we lose track of who we really are. We lose our *selves*.

Talking Things Over With Yourself

There's a simple way you can start claiming your feelings, future dreams, and needs. We call it *Talking Things Over With Yourself.* Here's how it works:

1. Ask yourself, "How am I feeling today?" Then name a feeling you are having. Next, talk it over with yourself. Your talk might go like this:

SAY...	**ASK...**
"I'm feeling sad today."	
	"Why am I feeling sad? What's happened that I feel sad about?"
"I'm feeling sad because I had an argument with my dad last night."	
	"What can I do about my sad feeling?"
"I can talk to my dad about the argument."	

Sometimes you can't change a feeling. But you can still talk it over with yourself. This is always better than pushing it away or locking it up inside.

Then we argued and he yelled "NEVER!" And now I feel so sad... What can I do about this feeling?

2. Ask yourself, "What are my future dreams?" Then name a dream for the near future or the far future. Next, talk it over with yourself. Your talk might go like this:

SAY...   **ASK...**

"I really want to work
with animals someday."

                                    "What do I have to learn to
                                    make this dream happen?"

"I can start by reading
books about people who
work with animals."

                                    "What will I actually do?"

"I can talk to pet doctors
and animal trainers to
find out."

3. Ask yourself, "Is there anything I need right now?" If yes, try to name your need. Then talk it over with yourself. Your talk might go like this:

SAY...   **ASK...**

"I need to make friends at
school. I feel left out and
lonely sometimes."

                                    "How can I start making
                                    friends?"

"I can ask if anyone wants
to shoot baskets with me
at recess."

                                    "What if nobody says yes?"

"I can find another group
of kids who are shooting
baskets. I can ask if it's
okay to play with them."

Sometimes you can't get what you need. But you can still talk it over with yourself. This is always better than pushing your need away or locking it up inside yourself.

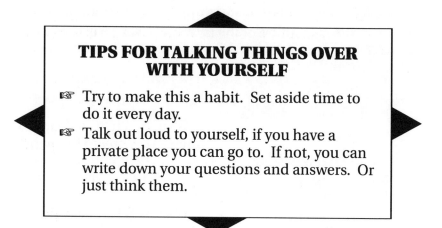

TIPS FOR TALKING THINGS OVER WITH YOURSELF

☞ Try to make this a habit. Set aside time to do it every day.

☞ Talk out loud to yourself, if you have a private place you can go to. If not, you can write down your questions and answers. Or just think them.

Great Escapes

Sometimes feelings are too strong to handle. Especially the ones that don't feel good. We get so distressed or fearful, ashamed or angry that the feeling takes us over.

At times like these, we need a way to escape from our feeling. We need a way to "step outside" of our feeling and let it go.

Here are four Great Escapes you can try.

1. Find something to laugh about

Read your favorite cartoon book. Watch a silly TV show. Ask somebody to tickle you or tell you a joke.

Maybe you can even find something funny about what's bothering you. We know a man who does this. He used to drop and break things a lot. He felt angry at himself for being clumsy. He felt ashamed because other people knew about him. He was often fearful that he would drop and break something else. One day he found a way to laugh at his problem. Now, whenever he drops something, he says, "Uh-oh! Gravity strikes again!"

2. Turn your attention to something besides your feeling

Go swimming or bicycling. Shoot some baskets or lace up your skates. Take a walk and concentrate on the sights and sounds around you.

Talk to yourself about everything you are seeing, hearing, smelling, and touching. This is a good way to let go of feeling shy, embarrassed, or ashamed.

3. Meditate

Meditation is another way to turn your attention to something besides a strong feeling. There are many different ways to meditate. Here's one you can try.

Bubble Meditation

☞ Find a quiet place where you can be alone for a while. Sit comfortably and close your eyes.

☞ Picture yourself holding a huge bubble wand and a bottle of bubble soap. You dip your wand into the soap. You start blowing big rainbow bubbles. They float away, getting smaller and smaller, and finally disappear.

☞ Put a worry inside each bubble. Watch your worry float away and disappear.

☞ Do this for five or ten minutes. Stop when you feel ready.

4. Daydream

Daydreams are like owning your favorite movies on video. You can watch them as many times as you want, for free!

You may already have your own special daydream for times when you need to "get away." Here are two more you can try.

"If I Could Have Whatever I Wanted..."

Sometimes we have strong feelings because we're pushing away or locking up another feeling, a future dream, or a need. This daydream can help you find out. Here are two examples.

— "If I could have whatever I wanted...someone would adopt my brothers and sisters and take them away!" Maybe you're feeling jealous of them. Maybe you have the need to feel different and separate. What can you do to get your need met?

— "If I could have whatever I wanted…my mom would rock me like she used to when I was a baby." Maybe you're feeling sad or fearful. Maybe you have the need for some touching and holding. What can you do to get your need met?

If you can't figure out what a daydream is telling you, try talking it over with an adult you trust. Maybe he or she can help you figure it out.

Facing Your Monster

Sometimes the best way to escape from something is to turn around and face it! This daydream helps you face the "monster" of your strong feeling.

☞ Think about your feeling. Maybe it's fear or anger, shame or jealousy. Maybe it's sadness or loneliness.

☞ Now imagine what your feeling "looks" like.

— Maybe fear looks like a tiny mouse. The mouse is shaking and its whiskers are quivering.

— Maybe anger looks like a creature made of fire. Smoke is coming out of its ears and nose!

— Maybe sadness looks like a blue elephant. Its ears and trunk and tail are hanging down.

☞ Now imagine yourself bringing your feeling a present. If your fear looks like a mouse, you could bring it a piece of cheese. If your anger looks like a fire creature, you could bring it an ice-cream cone. If your sadness looks like a blue elephant, you could bring it some pink peanuts.

This daydream might even make you laugh!

GETTING AND USING POWER IN YOUR RELATIONSHIPS AND YOUR LIFE

Lisa can't wait to grow up. Maybe then she'll finally have some power over her own life!

Right now it seems like everybody else gets to order her around. If she doesn't want to do something, she has to do it anyway, or she has to take the "consequences." She hates that word, "consequences." She hears it a thousand times a day!

Her mom orders her to make her bed. If she doesn't do it, the "consequences" are no TV. Her dad orders her to walk the dog. If she doesn't do it, the "consequences" are a 10-minute time out. Her teacher orders her to write a report. If she doesn't do it, first she gets a low grade, and then she gets in trouble at home.

Plus there are other people who get to tell her what to do. The babysitter. Her big brother. Her Sunday-school teacher. Her gymnastics coach. Her piano teacher. Even her neighbor, Mrs. Evans. Last week, Mrs. Evans told her to stop bouncing her ball outside the apartment.

Lisa wishes there could be just one day *when she got to give the orders. She would make everybody sorry!*

It's tough being a kid, and that's the truth. Anybody who tells you "this is the best time of your life" needs a head examination!

What's so great about it, anyway? You're short. You can't drive. You have to go to school. You have to ask permission to go to the bathroom! Other people tell you to clean your room or wash your ears. You have to live where they say, eat what they say, even say what they say sometimes. It's the pits!

In fact, you have more power than you think. And you can use this power to stick up for yourself.

Two Kinds of Power

There are two kinds of power you should know about: *role power* and *personal power.*

Role power is "built in" to certain roles or jobs. Parents have role power over their kids. They get to make rules, give privileges, take privileges away, and more *just because they're parents.*

Teachers have role power over their students. They get to give assignments and tests, raise or lower grades, keep kids after school, and more *just because they're teachers.*

Many other people have role power. Like babysitters, Scout leaders, principals, and coaches. Police officers, law makers, judges, and presidents.

You might even have some role power yourself. If you're the leader of a club, head of the student council, or first chair in the school orchestra, then you have role power. You get to make decisions other people don't, *just because* of your role.

Role power and personal power are NOT the same. Here are some of the ways they're different:

- ▶ Role power is something you get "just because." Personal power is something you get because you *want it* and you *work for it.*
- ▶ Role power depends on having someone else to be powerful over. (A king without people to rule doesn't have much role power.) Personal power depends on you and only you.
- ▶ Role power is something you might have to wait for.

You might never have very much role power. Personal power is something you can have *right now,* if you want it. And you can have as much as you want.

▸ Only some people can have role power. Anyone can have personal power. You can have personal power. *Even if many people have role power over you.*

It's important to understand these differences. Some people spend their whole lives fighting back against other people with role power. And some people think that role power is the only kind of power worth having. This causes problems in their lives.

Go back to page 51 and read Lisa's story again. Can you see why Lisa is having problems? She's angry with everyone who has role power in her life. She wishes she could get back at them. What a big waste of energy!

What can Lisa do instead? She can accept that some people have role power over her. She can work on building her personal power. Then she won't care so much that some people have role power over her. She'll feel secure and confident inside herself anyway.

If you're always fighting back against people who have role power over you, is it doing any good? Probably not. It might even be getting you in trouble.

Here's an idea: Stop fighting back. Accept that some people have role power over you. Use your energy to build personal power. This is a way to stick up for yourself.

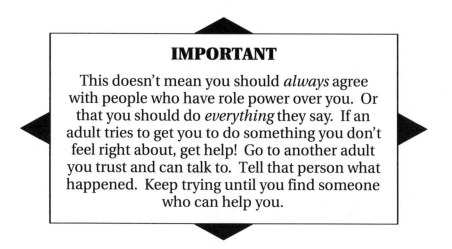

IMPORTANT

This doesn't mean you should *always* agree with people who have role power over you. Or that you should do *everything* they say. If an adult tries to get you to do something you don't feel right about, get help! Go to another adult you trust and can talk to. Tell that person what happened. Keep trying until you find someone who can help you.

Power In Your Relationships

••••••••••••••••••••━━━━━••••••••••••••••••

Evan and Dean live in the same neighborhood. Evan is in fourth grade. Dean is in sixth grade. One day Evan is riding his skateboard on the sidewalk when Dean walks by.

"That's a cool skateboard," Dean says.

Evan is surprised that a big kid is talking to him, but he says, "Thanks. I got it for my birthday."

"I have a skateboard, too," Dean says. "I can show you some tricks, if you want."

"Okay," Evan answers.

Dean gets his skateboard. For the next hour, the two boys skateboard together. Evan has a lot of fun. He likes Dean. And he wants Dean to like him, too.

••••••••••••••━━━━━•••••••••••••••••••••••••

Whenever we care what someone else thinks of us, we give that person power over us. We act in ways we believe that person will like. We start looking up to that person and copying him or her.

Evan cares what Dean thinks of him. That's okay as long as Dean treats Evan with respect. There are things Evan can learn from Dean. He can become a better skateboarder. But what if Dean doesn't treat Evan with respect? Maybe he makes fun of Evan or tries to teach him tricks that are too hard for him. That's *not* okay!

All through your life, you'll meet people whose opinions matter to you. You'll want them to like you, and you'll give them power over you. How will you know if they're treating you with respect? Pay attention to your feelings. If being with them and learning from them feels good and right inside, then do it! If it feels bad and wrong inside, or if it feels uncomfortable or funny, then don't do it.

You'll also meet people who care about what *you* think of *them*. This will make you feel powerful. How will you know if you're treating them with respect? Pay attention to your feelings. You'll know when you're acting in ways that are good for them — and when you're not.

Power and Choice

· ·

Beth is reading a book when her mom comes home from work.

"Have you done your chores yet?" her mom wants to know.

"Not yet," Beth answers. "I got interested in this book."

"Put it down RIGHT NOW," her mom orders. "Do your chores RIGHT NOW or you'll be grounded for a week!"

Shannon is watching TV when her mom comes home from work.

"Have you done your chores yet?" her mom wants to know.

"Not yet," Shannon answers. "I wanted to watch this program first."

"Shannon, we have a problem," her mom says. "You're supposed to do your chores when you come home from school."

"But this is my favorite program!" Shannon exclaims.

"I understand that. So let's see if we can find an answer to our problem."

Her mom thinks for a few moments. Then she says, "Maybe you can do your chores before you leave for school in the morning. Then you can watch your program when you get home. Or you can use the VCR to record your program while you do your chores. Then you can watch it later in the evening. Which do you choose?"

"I don't want to do my chores in the morning," Shannon says. "I guess I'll record the program and watch it later."

Her mom smiles. "Let's try it for a few days and see how it works."

Beth and Shannon both have chores to do after school. In this way, they are the same. But Beth feels powerless while Shannon feels powerful. Why? Because Beth's mom gave her an order, and Shannon's mom gave her a choice.

Whenever we are given a choice, we feel powerful. Many parents and other people with role power know this. They try to give kids choices. Even if these are "little" choices, like "Do you want the good-tasting medicine first? Or do you want the bad-tasting medicine first?" The child can't choose whether or not to take the bad-tasting medicine. But he or she can choose *when* to take it. This helps the child feel powerful instead of powerless.

If you feel powerless at home, maybe you can talk to your parents. Tell them how you feel. Ask if they can give you choices sometimes. This is a way to stick up for yourself.

Then, when you make a choice, do what you say you will do! For example, what if Shannon watches her program and doesn't do her chores? Her mom might decide to take away her choice.

What if your parents won't give you choices? Even then, you don't have to be powerless. *You can give yourself choices.* Here are two you can think about:

- ▶ You can choose to accept things the way they are. If your parents don't want to change, you can't make them.
- ▶ You can choose to do a Great Escape. This will help if you're feeling angry, sad, ashamed, or just frustrated. You'll find some Great Escapes on pages 48–50.

Equal Power

• •
■■■■■■■■

Mike and Dennis live in the same apartment building. They often play together. They get along pretty well — as long as Mike does what Dennis wants. If he doesn't, Dennis threatens to go home! When this happens, Mike feels powerless. He doesn't want Dennis to go home. So he gives in.

■■■■■■■■
• •

Dennis has all the power in this relationship. He uses it to get his own way. But there is something Mike can do to stick up for himself. The next time Dennis threatens to go home, Mike can smile and say, "See you later!"

This will really surprise Dennis. Maybe he'll leave anyway. But maybe he'll stay. Mike will just have to wait and find out.

By *not* giving in to Dennis, Mike will take back some of the power Dennis had all to himself. The two boys will now have equal power.

• •
▬▬▬▬▬▬▬

Julie and Colette are friends. They enjoy playing together. But sometimes Julie promises she will come to Colette's house, and then she doesn't come. So Colette waits and waits. Finally she calls Julie on the phone. Then Julie says something like, "I'm sorry, I forgot." Or "I decided to stay home." Or "Ann came over and I'm playing with her instead."

When this happens, Colette feels powerless. She keeps expecting Julie to keep her promises. She feels hurt, ashamed, and angry when Julie breaks her promises.

▬▬▬▬▬▬▬
• •

Julie has all the power in this relationship. Colette can't change Julie's behavior, but she can stick up for herself. Here are some things she can try:

▶ **Colette can find more friends.** Then she won't depend on Julie so much.

▶ **Colette can go to Julie's house instead of calling her on the phone.** Maybe Julie will want to play with her. But maybe she won't. Colette will have to wait and see.

▶ **Colette can stop expecting Julie to keep her promises.** We *should* be able to expect our friends to keep their promises. But Julie has broken a lot of promises! So this isn't a realistic expectation for Colette to have.

By *not* expecting Julie to keep her promises, Colette can take back some of the power Julie had all to herself. The two girls will have equal power.

Power In Your Life

Even though you're "just a kid," you're a powerful person! Just think of the things you can do:

▶ **You can be responsible for your behavior and your feelings.** Nobody can make you do things you know you shouldn't do. Nobody can make you feel mad or sad, fearful or ashamed.

▶ **You can make choices about your behavior and your feelings.** You can decide to be the kind of person other people can count on. You can choose to feel good about yourself. You can learn to make wise choices and have realistic expectations.

CHOICE = POWER

▶ **You can name and claim your feelings.** You can tell other people how you feel. You can stick up for your feelings.

▶ **You can name and claim your future dreams.** You can decide what is important to you. You can stick up for your future dreams and work to make them come true.

▶ **You can name and claim your needs.** You can understand your needs. You can stick up for your needs and work to get them met.

▶ **You can take a Great Escape when your feelings get too strong to handle.** You can "step outside" your feelings and let them go.

▶ **You can get power in your relationships with other people.** You can make choices so you won't feel powerless. You can try to get equal power in some of your relationships.

All of these things add up to **personal power**. You can use your personal power in all parts of your life. You can feel secure and confident inside no matter where you are, who you are with, or what you are doing. With personal power, you really are in charge of your own life!

HOW TO LIVE HAPPILY EVER AFTER

Here is how it happens in fairy tales: A poor, powerless man turns out to be a king, marries a princess, and they live happily ever after. Or a poor, powerless woman gets noticed by a prince, they marry, and the two of them live happily ever after.

It would be great if things worked out that way in real life. But they don't. In fact, there's no such thing as "living happily ever after."

You are responsible for your own happiness. Other people can care about your happiness, but no one else can *make* you happy. Only you can choose how you face life and how you feel about yourself. And even you can't make yourself happy all of the time.

We live in a culture that tells us to *expect* happiness. If we aren't happy, then there must be something wrong with us! But this isn't a realistic expectation. Real life is full of surprises. You'll have good days and bad days. You'll be happy sometimes and sad sometimes.

What you can do is learn to *collect and store* happiness so you always have a supply. There's a way to do this that works for *everyone* who tries it.

The Happiness List

Some people store good feelings inside themselves and let go of bad ones. Other people do just the opposite. Which kind are you? Here's a way to find out:

> *Right now, write down five things that happened yesterday. These should be the first five things that come to your mind.*

When you finish writing, read your list. Did you remember five good things, five bad things, or some of each?

You can choose what things to remember. You can learn to remember good feelings and let go of bad ones. Here's how:

☞ **Right now, write down five things that happened today which you feel good about.**

These don't have to be Big Things. If you wait to get straight A's or win a million dollars, you may never get to write! Instead, think about the small things you usually don't notice that put a smile on your face.

Did the sun shine today? Did your teacher give you a compliment? Did you get to pet a puppy? Were your new shoes comfy? Did a friend let you borrow a favorite toy? These could all go on your Happiness List.

☞ **Do this EVERY DAY. Weekdays and weekends. School days and holidays.**

You can do it before you go to bed at night. Or you can keep a notebook in your pocket and do it throughout the day.

It won't always be easy to remember good things. There will be days when you really have to work at it. But don't give up. You can do it!

Why is it so important to make a Happiness List every day? There are five reasons (and maybe more):

1. It boosts your *personal power*.
2. It teaches you that *you are responsible* for your own happiness.

3. It teaches you that *you can choose* how to experience your life.
4. It teaches you to look for things which *create* happiness.
5. It teaches you how to *collect and store* good feelings.

Think of this as a "happiness savings account." The next time you feel sad or depressed, angry or fearful, you can go to your "savings account," take out a good feeling, and actually *feel* it all over again. This will turn your attention away from your bad feeling.

HOW TO MAKE THE MOST OF YOUR HAPPINESS LIST

☞ Do it with a parent or your whole family. This is a great habit for everyone to get into!

☞ Keep your Happiness Lists in a special notebook or folder. Decorate your notebook or folder any way you choose.

☞ Every so often, read through your Happiness Lists and enjoy your good feelings all over again.

☞ Every so often, look through your Happiness Lists and pick something to experience all over again. For example: If you wrote, "I took a walk with my mom," invite her to take another walk with you. If you wrote, "I saw the sunset," watch the sunset again.

LEARNING TO LIKE YOURSELF

....

An alien has just landed in your back yard! But instead of saying, "Take me to your leader," the alien pulls out a laser gun and points it at you.

Then the alien says, "Yuck! A human! I don't like humans very much. Humans are loud. Humans are messy. Humans are wasteful! I can't think of a single good thing about them."

The laser gun hums. The alien stops and thinks for a moment. Then it says, "I usually blow humans into molecules. But I am going to give you a chance to talk me out of it.

"You have one minute to tell me five good things about yourself. Then maybe — just maybe — I will not blow you into molecules."

The laser gun lowers. The alien waits. What will you say????

....

Can you think of five good things about yourself? Five things you really like about yourself?

Do you have enough self-esteem?

To stick up for yourself, you need personal power *and* positive self-esteem. *You need to believe you are worth sticking up for.*

How would you rate YOUR self-esteem?

LISTENING TO YOUR INNER VOICES: A SELF-ESTEEM SELF-QUIZ

DIRECTIONS

For each question, pick the response that is *closest* to the way you talk to yourself, think about yourself, or feel inside yourself.

1. When you get up in the morning and look at yourself in the mirror, what do you say?

    a. "You look great this morning! And you're about to have a great day."

    b. "Oh, no, not you again! Why do you even bother to get out of bed?"

2. When you fail at something or make a big mistake, what do you tell yourself?

    a. "Everyone has the right to fail or make mistakes every day."

    b. "You blew it again! You can't do *anything* right! You should have known better."

3. When you succeed at something, what do you say to yourself?

    a. "Congratulations! You should be proud of yourself."

    b. "You could have done better, if you had tried harder."

4. You have just talked to someone who has role power over you. (Like a parent, a teacher, or a coach.) What do you tell yourself?

    a. "You handled that pretty well."

    b. "You acted so stupid! You *always* say dumb things."

5. You have just left the first meeting of a club you joined. What do you say to yourself?

    a. "That was fun. You met some new people you liked. They even laughed at the joke you told."

    b. "You talked too much, and nobody liked you. Everybody hated your joke."

6. You have just left a friend's house after playing together. What do you tell yourself?

    a. "That was fun. Your friend really likes you!"

    b. "Your friend was just pretending to like you. You probably won't get invited back ever again."

7. When someone gives you a compliment or says, "I like you," what do you say to yourself?

    a. "You deserve it!"

    b. "Nobody gives you a compliment unless they want something back. Besides, you don't deserve it."

8. When someone you care about lets you down, what do you tell yourself?

    a. "Your feelings are hurt, but you'll get over it. Later you can try to find out what happened."

    b. "This proves that person doesn't care about you."

9. When you let down someone you care about, what do you say to yourself?

    a. "It isn't nice, and it isn't fun, but sometimes people let each other down. Admit what you did and get on with your life."

    b. "How could you do such a terrible thing? You should be ashamed of yourself."

10. When you feel needy or unsure of yourself, what do you tell yourself?

    a. "Everybody feels this way sometimes. Get a hug from your mom or curl up with your blanket, and you'll feel better soon."

    b. "Grow up! Don't be such a baby. That's disgusting!"

SCORING

Give yourself 10 points for every (a) answer and 5 points for every (b) answer.

Then use this key to find your Self-Esteem Rating:

KEY

90–100: Your self-esteem is HIGH and POSITIVE. (Read the rest of this book anyway.)

75–90: Your self-esteem COULD BE BETTER. We will tell you ways to raise it.

60–75: Your self-esteem is LOW. But now you know it, and you can choose to change.

50–60: Your self-esteem is DUST. The alien just blasted you to molecules. Luckily there's a Molecule Glue you can use. It's called the I-Did-It List.

The I-Did-It List

The I-Did-It List is like the Happiness List described on pages 62–63. But instead of writing down things that happened, you write down things you did.

Right now, write down five things you did yesterday.

When you're done writing, read your list. Did you remember five successes? Or five failures? Or some of each?

You can choose what things to remember for your I-Did-It List. Pick things you feel *proud* of. Like activities you took part in. Problems you solved. Successes you had. Accomplishments of any kind. And anything else you feel satisfied with and good about.

☞ **Right now, write down five things you did today which you feel proud of.**

At first it might be hard to think of even one. Keep trying! These don't have to be Big Successes. You don't have to win the Nobel Prize or climb Mount Everest. You don't have to be a hero or a star.

You'll find that you do great things when you are just being yourself. Your list might include things like this:

1. I made my bed without being told.
2. I got to school on time.
3. I knew 8 out of 10 answers on the math test.
4. When our hamster got out of its cage, I helped find it.
5. I set the table for dinner.

☞ **Do this EVERY DAY. Weekdays and weekends. School days and holidays.**

Why is it good to keep an I-Did-It List? It helps you stick up for yourself *with yourself.* Sometimes you might forget that you are valuable and worthwhile. The I-Did-It List reminds you. It gives you proud feelings every day.

Think of your I-Did-It List as a "self-esteem savings account." Use it like your "happiness savings account."

For more tips on what to do with your I-Did-It List, see "How To Make The Most Of Your Happiness List" on page 63. You can use the same ideas for your I-Did-It List.

SELF-ESTEEM DO'S AND DON'TS

☞ *DO get in the habit of positive feeling and thinking.*

When you have a negative or critical thought about yourself, change it into a positive thought. When your inner voices say something mean to you, talk back!

CHANGE THIS...	INTO THIS...
I can't do anything right.	I can build a great campfire.
Nobody wants to be my friend.	I can be a friend to someone.
I am so stupid sometimes!	I know a lot about airplanes.
What if nobody likes my science fair project?	I am proud of my science fair project.

It will take time before this feels natural. For some adults, it can take a year or more. We believe kids learn faster than adults. So maybe it won't take that long for you.

☞ *DON'T worry so much about what other people think of you.* Instead, decide what you think of them!

Most of us feel anxious about meeting new people. We wonder, "What will they think of me? Will they like me? Will they think I'm dumb? Will they think I'm boring?" That kind of thinking makes us more anxious. It makes us powerless, self-conscious, and ashamed.

You can choose to change your thinking around. You can wonder, "What will I think of them? Will I like them? Will I think they're interesting?" Then you have equal power and no shame.

☞ *DO keep being yourself.*

Remember that the person you are is good enough. Be pleased and proud of the person you are.

☞ *DON'T ever question your basic worth as a human being.*

Every human being is worthwhile. That includes you!

☞ *DO treat yourself like a worthwhile person.*

Give yourself plenty of praise — not just for the things you do, but for who you are and how you live your life.

☞ *DON'T blame yourself when things go wrong in life.* And DON'T accept any blame that others try to put on you, even adults.

Remember that you are responsible for *your own* behavior and *your own* feelings. It isn't "your fault" if your mom gets angry. It isn't "your fault" if your softball team loses the game.

☞ *DO expect to make mistakes.*

We believe that every human being has the right to make FOUR BIG MISTAKES every day. That includes you!

☞ *DON'T compare yourself to other people.*

This is a hard habit to break. We live in a culture that teaches us to compare. Parents compare their children. Schools compare their students.

Remember that you're different and special. You're one of a kind. There's nobody in the world exactly like you.

☞ *DO give yourself permission to fail.*

Just because you fail at something doesn't mean *you* are a failure. Everybody fails sometimes. Nobody's perfect.

☞ *DO make Happiness Lists and I-Did-It Lists every day.* They really will help you to collect and store good feelings and self-esteem.

SIX GOOD THINGS TO DO FOR YOURSELF

1. Choose something to do *just for fun*. Then do it whenever you can.

Go swimming, go swinging, build models. Paint pictures, play basketball, draw cartoons. Write stories, be a clown, learn to use a computer. And forget the old saying, "Anything worth doing is worth doing well." Don't try to be perfect, ever. Don't try to be an expert at everything. Keep some things just for fun.

2. Give yourself a "present" every day.

This can be almost anything, as long as it's *just for you*. Listen to your favorite tape. Take a bubble bath. Play with your LEGOs. Learn a joke.

3. Forgive yourself for something you did in the past.

We've all done things we wish we hadn't done. We've all hurt someone else's feelings. But we don't have to feel sad, guilty, or ashamed forever.

Pick something you did in the past. Remember it one last time. Think about everything that happened. What were the consequences? Did you get punished? Now close your eyes, give yourself a hug, and say, "I forgive myself."

4. Do at least one thing every day that's good for your body.

Take a walk or do some sit-ups. Eat fresh vegetables or fruit. Wash your hair. Floss your teeth.

5. Do at least one thing every day that's good for your brain.

Solve a puzzle or do a brain-teaser. Read a book. Memorize part of a poem. Listen to a concert on the radio. Look at an art book.

6. Find an adult you can trust and talk to.

Being a kid is scary sometimes. An adult can help you face your fears. Being a kid is confusing sometimes. An adult can help answer your questions. Maybe not *all* of them, but at least some of them!

Let your feelings guide you to the right person. Pick someone you feel safe with. Pick someone who cares enough to listen and tries to understand how you feel. This is one of the *best* things you can ever do for yourself.

LOOKING BACK AT THE BEGINNING: HOW PETER, TARA, AND SAM CAN STICK UP FOR THEMSELVES

Do you remember Peter, Tara, and Sam? Peter got teased at school. Tara's parents blamed her for everything. Sam's study hall teacher wasn't fair. You can read their stories again on page ix.

Imagine that Peter, Tara, and Sam know the ideas you have been learning in this book. They know about personal power and positive self-esteem. They know how to stick up for themselves. Here is how their stories might continue.

. . . .

The next time the other kids tease him, Peter looks them straight in the eye and says, "Even if you think so, I don't. And my opinion is the only one that counts. I know myself a lot better than you do." Peter knows not to give anyone else the power to determine how he feels about himself.

The next time Tara's parents blame her for something, Tara looks them straight in the eye and says, "I do the best I can. I'm not perfect." Later she asks her parents if they were ever blamed by their parents. She asks them how they felt as children when that happened to them. Tara listens. Then she says, "That's how I feel when you blame me."

*Sam returns to school the next day and asks to
speak privately to his study hall teacher. He starts
by saying, "I admit I broke the rule about not talking. But could you listen to my side of the story?"
Then he calmly explains about Troy kicking him.
He asks if he can be seated somewhere else, away
from Troy.*

*Before leaving, Sam asks his teacher one more
question: "If the same thing happens again, what
can I do so I don't break the rule?" Sam feels stronger
because he knows how to stick up for himself.*

• • • • • • • • • • • • • • • • ▬▬▬▬▬ • • • • • • • • • • • • • • • •

When you have personal power, you feel confident and you
can make choices. When you have positive self-esteem, you
value the person you are, no matter what.

Personal power and positive self-esteem are skills you can
learn, like reading, writing, and arithmetic. Because you have
learned them, you can be like Peter, Tara, and Sam. You can
stick up for yourself, starting today!

INDEX

A

Accomplishments, listing of, 68–69
Adults, trust of, 74
Ambivalent feelings, 30
Anger, feelings of, 24–25
Anguish, feelings of, 22–23
Assertiveness
    about feelings, 59
    personal power and, 1, 75–76
    role power and, 52–53

B

Behavior
    accepting consequences of, 4–6, 51
    choices about, 8–10
    responsibility for, 2–6, 59
Belonging, need for, 39
Brain teasers, 73
Bubble meditation, 49

C

Change, in goals and dreams, 33–36
Childhood, memories of, 32–33
Choice
    decisions about, 8–10
    parent's desires and, 14
    personal power and, 1, 55–57, 59
    reality and expectations about, 10–13
Combination feelings, 30
Comparisons, avoidance of, 72
Compliments, importance of, 43
Confrontation, feelings and, 50–51
Contempt, feeling of, 28

D

Daydreaming, 49–50
Decision-making skills, choices and, 8–10
Depression, identification of, 16
Disgust, feeling of, 29
Distress, feelings of, 22

E

Enjoyment, feelings of, 19
Equality, personal power and, 57–58
Escaping from feelings, 48–50
Excitement, as feeling, 18–19
Exercise, as release from feeling, 49
Expectations, reality and, 10–13

F

Fearfulness, feelings of, 23
Feelings
    assertiveness about, 59
    basic types of, listed, 17
    choices about, 8–10
    combinations of, 30
    confronting, 50–51
    diversion from, 49
    escape from, 48–50
    expressing, 31
    identification of, 15–17, 44–45
    judgments about, 17, 31, 45
    responsibility for, 6–7
    self–discussion about, 46–48
    sharing with others, 10
    triggers for, 6–7
    vocabulary of, 17–29
Forgiveness, of self, 73
Friendship
    equality and, 57–58
    personal power, 54–55
    realistic expectations about, 12–13

Fun, importance of, 73
Future dreams, *see* Goals

G

Goals
    assertiveness about, 59
    during childhood, 32–33
    future changes in, 34–35
    identification of, 44–45
    in present, 33–34
    techniques for setting, 33–36
Great escapes technique, 48–50
Grief, dealing with, 10

H

Happiness, responsibility for, 61
Happiness List, 62–63
"Happiness savings account,"
    62–63
Health, importance of, 73
High-intensity feelings, 17
Humiliation, feeling of, 27
Humor, as emotional release, 48

I

"I-Did-It List," 68–69
Imaging techniques, feelings
    and, 50
Interest, as feeling, 18

J

Jealousy, identification of, 16
Joy, feelings of, 19

L

Laughter, 48
Low-intensity feelings, 17

M

Meditation, 49
Misery, feelings of, 22–23

N

Need(s)
    assertiveness about, 59
    for belonging, 39
    identification of, 36–45
    for nurturing, 41–42
    for power in relationships and
        life, 43–44
    for relationships, 37
    self-discussion about, 46–48
    for self-worth, 42–43
    for touching and holding, 38
    for uniqueness, 40
    wants and, 36
Nurturing, need for, 41–42

P

Parental pressure, 14
    choice and personal power,
        55–57
    role power and, 52–53
Patience, personal power and, 9
Perfectionism
    assertiveness and, 75–76
    vs. responsibility, 6
Personal power
    choices and, 55–57, 59
    defined, 1, 12
    equality and, 57–58
    naming feelings and, 15–17
    need for, 43–44
    relationships and, 54–55
Popularity, overemphasis on, 14
"Presents," to yourself, 73
Promises, importance of, 58

R

Rage, feelings of, 25
Realistic expectations
   choices and, 10–13
   equality and, 57–58
Relationships
   need for, 37
   personal power and, 1, 43–44,
     54–55
Responsibility
   abdication of, 3–6
   vs. control, 2
   for feelings, 6–7
   for personal behavior, 2–6
   for personal happiness, 61
   personal power and, 1–6
Role power, 52–53

S

Self-esteem
   decision-making and, 9
   do's and don'ts, 70–72
   rating guidelines for, 65–66
   self-quiz, 66–68
Self-knowledge, 14–15, 46–48
   personal power and, 1
Self, loss of, 45
Self-worth, 70–71
   need for, 42–43
Shame
   identifying, 26
   self-esteem and, 70
Shock, feelings of, 21
Success, overemphasis on, 12–13
Surprise, feelings of, 20–21

T

Teachers, role power and, 52–53
Teasing, assertiveness and,
   75–76
Terror, feelings of, 24

Tomkins, Silvan (Dr.), 17
Touching and holding, need for,
   38
Trust, in adults, 74

U

Uniqueness, need for, 40

W

Wants, needs and, 36

About The Authors

Gershen Kaufman was educated at Columbia University and received his Ph.D. in clinical psychology from the University of Rochester. Currently he is a professor in the Counseling Center at Michigan State University. He is also the author of *Shame: The Power of Caring* (Cambridge, Massachusetts: Schenkman Books, Inc., 1985) and *The Psychology of Shame: Theory and Treatment of Shame-Based Syndromes* (New York: Springer Publishing Co., 1989). He is the coauthor with Lev Raphael of *Dynamics of Power: Building a Competent Self* (Cambridge, Massachusetts: Schenkman Books, Inc., 1983).

Lev Raphael was educated at Fordham University and received his MFA in Creative Writing from the University of Massachusetts at Amherst. He holds a Ph.D. in American Studies from Michigan State University, where he has taught as an assistant professor of American Thought and Language. A prize-winning writer, he has published over two dozen short stories in magazines including *Redbook, Commentary,* and *Midstream.* With Gershen Kaufman, he co-developed and co-taught the program, "Psychological Health and Self-Esteem," on which *Dynamics of Power: Building a Competent Self* and this book are based.

May we introduce other Free Spirit materials you will find helpful...

Fighting Invisible Tigers:
A Stress Management Guide For Teens
Earl Hipp

Dreams Can Help:
A Journal Guide to Understanding Your Dreams
and Making Them Work For You
Jonni Kincher

Writing Down The Days:
365 Creative Journaling Ideas For Young People
Lorraine M. Dahlstrom

FREE SPIRIT: News & Views On Growing Up
Editors: Judy Galbraith and Pamela Espeland

Please write or call for a free copy of our catalog:

Free Spirit Publishing, Inc.
400 First Avenue North, Suite 616
Minneapolis, MN 55401
(612) 338-2068